Leadership Mantras for Success

*Simple management lessons
for applying in real life situations*

KISHORE MURALIDHARAN

DEDICATION

Dedicated to all the wonderful people, who have made my life meaningful. I thank Junior Chamber International for giving me opportunities that have helped me to understand my potential.

Most of all, my wife Kala and my two angels Sharanya & Sharika.. They have made my world beautiful.

CONTENTS

Acknowledgments   i

1   About the Author   10

2   Blurbs   11

3   Introduction   14

4   Foreword   15

5   Communication   18

6   Communicating Expectations   19

7   Feedback Mechanism   20

8   Response   22

9   Self-pep-talk   24

10   Investing Time   26

11   Value of time   28

12   Being an Example   30

13   Facing problems head on   31

14   Challenge to think   32

15   Reward   34

16   Commitment   36

17   Evaluation   38

18   Planning   39

19 Innovation   41

20 Jugaad Innovation   43

21 Open to Ideas   45

22 The Kid in You   47

23 Crisis Management   48

24 Being a Salesman   50

25 Dreaming Success   52

26 Transparency   53

27 Be updated   55

28 Emotions   56

29 Integrity   57

30 Calculated Risk   58

31 Focus   61

32 At what cost?   63

33 Facing Criticism   64

34 Faith   65

35 Happiness   66

36 Energy Investment   68

37 Owning Responsibility   69

38 Nourish business relationship   71

39 What is your USP?   73

40	Celebrate Life	74
41	Winning Attitude	76
42	Failure is not a Villain	78
43	Be alone with your self	79
44	Travel with an open mind	80
45	Humility	82
46	Impart knowledge	84
47	Be a hero	85
48	Be Passionate	87
49	Back to Basics	88
50	Procrastination	90
51	Adaptability	91
52	The company we keep	92
53	Junk in the Information Highway	94
54	Understanding entrepreneurship	96
55	Look back	98
56	Scalability	100
57	Walk the talk	102
58	Freedom	105
59	Criticism is good	107
60	Future Ready	110

61	Power of silence	112
62	Self Motivation	114
63	Respect Nature	116
64	The Mentor	118
65	The Guru	120
66	Specialisation	123
67	Fear and Anxiety	125
68	Friends we keep	126
69	Hire and Fire	128
70	People and Change	129
71	Subtract to Add	130
72	Peer Pressure	132

ACKNOWLEDGMENTS

I had been planning to write a book on simple management for the common man; since a very long time ,I wanted to put my 26 years of learning from various business organisations into a book,which would benefit young entrepreneurs and future business leaders. I could never have done this without the support of my friends from the Junior Chamber International. JCI is an international organisation which believes that the earth's great treasure lies in human personality ,JCI has helped millions of young people to sharpen their knowledge and create a positive change in them. I had been sharing "management tips" and "success mantras" on social media for a very long time and all my friends encouraged me to put those mantras & tips into a book for all to read .In this book I have compiled few of the mantras and tried to create a simple book which could be read in a very casual manner and yet convey management lessons in snippets.

I wish to thank Dr.Raghavan IRS for readily agreeing to write a foreword for my book. Dr Raghavan has been an inspiration to me. His books the **Dividing Lines** *: Contours of India China Conflict,* **Vanishing Shangri La** *: History of Tibet and Dalai Lamas in 20th century are works of his well researched effort. Dr.V.N.S Pillai has contributed some wonderful ideas which I have incorporated in this work. Dr.Pillai and Mrs Gopika Sreekaran helped me in re arranging the words of my book into a good reading material, I thank both of them for this great help in editing my book . Advocate Vaman Kumar is my training Guru he was my coach at National Train the Trainers Workshop.I acknowledge the support of my well wishers Harish Kumar,Nibu John, Shibu Damodar, Dr,Harish, Rajesh Panicker, Manoj Govind and all my friends from JCI Cochin Trainers Forum.*

1 ABOUT THE AUTHOR

With over a quarter century experience in sales and marketing operations, in India and abroad, Kishore Kumar Muralidharan is currently Managing Director of Fiesta Rubber & Latex Technologies Pvt.Ltd. and the India Representative of Crusader Chemical Co Inc., Baltimore, USA. He is a certified National Trainer of JC International and NLP Trainer. He has many innovations to his credit like training 25000 girl students of fifty schools in self-defence. As a practicing manager and a sought after management speaker Kishore Kumar Muralidharan is giving here useful tips for business owners, managers / management students.

2 BLURBS

Brevity is the need of the hour. Time is at a premium in this fast paced world. One topic after another, in a simple capsule form, everyday morning, through whatsapp, has been a welcome positive kick right in the morning. Happy that Mr Kishore kumar has compiled them and bringing it out as a book 'Leadership Manrtras for Success'. I am sure this will serve as a quick reference material for young entrepreneurs and trainers. Hearty Congratulation and all the very best Mr.Kishore.Muralidharan.

Harishkumar
CorporateTrainer
Winner of Ravi Puraskar Award for the Outstanding Trainer of JCI India in 2015

Kishore kumar Muralidharan is a highly motivated leadership trainer. This book "Leadership Mantras For Success" is a reference book for busy Gen-X leaders of tomorrow. I personally consider the contents of this book as "deepest lessons in shortest sentences"

Rajesh Panicker, *Life Coach & Yoga Trainer*

A leader is one who always think about solutions. "Success Mantras" is a cute little guide which will serve any individual as to how to face and tackle leadership challenges, be it in organizational, professional or personal.

Jc.Dr.HarishKumar.H
ZonePresident,,JCIIndia,ZoneXX,Practicing.Homoeopath
National Trainer - JCI India

"This book is like a multivitamin capsule of management lessons, It is a one stop shop for young business entrepreneurs for most of their skill needs."

Jc Ramkumar Menon,*Editor – Challange,Past Executive Vice President JCI India.*

"You can read it at one go. Or progress one point a day. Any which way you approach it, you can be sure of one thing; it's a collection of practical snippets of wisdom amassed by a business leader and trainer, as a part of his fabulous career"

NibuJohn.
*President,JCIIndia,CochinChapter,AvertisingProfessional
National Trainer - JCI India*

"The debut from Mr.Kishore Mualidharan has come out excellent . The drawings of content give one more reason to approach the matters in a different perception. This is a novel approach to a BIG subject"

Manoj Govind.,*Executive Vice President,Next Best Solutions Pvt. Ltd*

This book is an excellent work of Kishore Muralidharan,it will help future leaders to gain knowledge of complex subject in the most simple manner.

Shibu Damodaran.*Corporate Trainer,Chief Trainer, Persona.*

The only true wisdom is in knowing you know nothing.

-Socrates

3 INTRODUCTION

Many books on management are written by professors who are 'people standing on the periphery of management'. Here is a book by Kishore Kumar Muralidharan, a practising manager, managing director of a company, who has over 25 years of exposure to sales and marketing. He is a sought after speaker on management and leadership. He was faculty at Life Insurance Insights, a higher level residential training programme for professors and professionals and his presentation on branding was highly appreciated by participants. Here in this book he has presented management/leadership concepts as small takeaways, which makes for lucid reading.

Dr.V.N.S.Pillai

Director, Life Insurance Insights & author 'Pension & Annuity', published by State Institute of Languages, Government of Kerala.

4 FOREWORD

Management has gained importance as a specialised area of study during the last three decades. The opening up of the economy and the unshackling of the forces of entrepreneurship within the country since 1991 created many opportunities for the new generation, both in terms of jobs available as well through new sectors that emerged. Simultaneously, there was a growing realisation that study of the principles of management in a systematic and organised manner is required for capitalising the gains on offer. This, in turn, led to an increased interest about this arena, both amongst students and professionals, leading to more research and writing on the topic. All aspects of management have been analysed in detail, propounded upon and brought into public domain during this period.

However, one finds that there has also been a tendency to complicate the subject by use of words and phrases which make its learning more difficult. Instead of making attempts to explain the subject in simple words to make it understood by even the uninitiated, it would appear that more efforts have been put into making the study of management more arduous and complex. This has resulted in study of management being considered as a elitist one, forgetting the basic fact that no other subject is as closely linked not only to business practices but to daily life, at all levels, than this speciality. In these circumstances, it is extremely heartening to note that Sri Kishore Muralidharan, the author of this book, has undertaken the noble task of explaining the basic tenets of management and leadership in simple language to the lay public.

Leadership skills constitute one of the most important elements involved in the making of a successful manager. While leadership styles differ from one leader to another, there are many common traits that all successful captains possess and demonstrate. They include ability to understand ones colleagues, motivate them, be one amongst his team, take decisions, stand by one's colleagues, take responsibility for any failure or lapse while being generous about sharing credit, promote free exchange of ideas and opinions without compromising discipline and above all, inculcate a culture of honesty within his team. A good leader would know that the critical aspect of his character would be the manner in which he responds to a crisis and would hence ensure that his actions do not result in spreading of panic amongst his team, in such situations. He would be required to think and act on the spot as well as to lay down the long term policies and goals of his organisation. In short, a leader is expected to be a master of all trades, besides being blessed with abundance of charisma, patience, benevolence and humanitarian spirit.

The formidable list of responsibilities that a leader has to discharge and the challenges he is required to tackle would make one think that no one less than a superman would be able to fit the bill. In real life one finds that, more often than not, individuals who are schooled in the rough and tumble of day to day life life emerge as more successful leaders than those who pass out from the best of business schools. The spirit of enterprise of such individuals along with the ingenuity, absolute faith and commitment to the cause and sheer audacity displayed by them at critical junctures mark them out as different from the rest of the pack. While they are worthy of adulation and reverence, it would not be advisable to emulate them as they are blessed with abilities that most others do not possess. Such individuals, who are not uniquely gifted by the Creator, stand to benefit from an insight into the basic canons of leadership.

Kishore Muralidharan has gained rich experience in the arena of management through his years of working in various capacities, as a manager, CEO, trainer, mentor and a public spirited individual, during the last two decades. This has helped him to break down the complex requirements of leadership and explain it in simple language with the help of examples that one would witness in daily life. This book can be defined as a well thought out effort to demystify the tenets of leadership and make them available for the masses in a language they can understand.

This book deserves to be read not only by aspiring managers but by all persons seeking to advance in life. I wish Kishore Muralidharan and his book all success.

Dr.K.N.Raghavan IRS,

Commissioner of Customs, Cochin.

Former,InternationalCricketUmpire,
Author of Books, **Dividing Lines** *: Contours of India China Conflict,*
Vanishing Shangri La *: History of Tibet and Dalai Lamas in 20th century*

4 COMMUNICATION

Communication is a tool to convey one's thoughts to others. Today there are many tools available to communicate; electronic media has made possible instant transmission of communication to thousands of people.

The emergence of mobile technology has opened a totally new medium for communication. The real challenge in using such technology lies in the ability to communicate with brevity. Every word we use in such medium should contribute to the message.
No amount of intelligence matters if one cannot communicate with clarity. Ensure that your message is conveyed without any ambiguity.

This requires good skill. Thank god, this skill can be developed through practice!

5 COMMUNICATING EXPECTATION

Successful leaders are great communicators; they encourage performance and motivate their team. This can happen only if the team knows what is expected of them.

Clarity in communication is very important in translating vision into mission and actionable objectives. Focus on your communication.

6 FEEDBACK MECHANISM

Feedback is an integral part of management communication. To make a great team, the right kind of feedback mechanism should be put in place.

It is often observed that timely feedbacks are not forthcoming and they are revealed only in the annual appraisal sheet. How can such feedback help your team leader / member? How can anyone move forward unless he knows where he has reached? And how much more effort he should put in to reach his goal?

The leader should ensure a continuous two-way flow of information between him and his team members. Such teams will succeed.

7 RESPONSE

We are always in responsive mode, our body and mind are alert to all external and internal stimuli. Based on these stimuli we tend to respond; it is this response that paves the way to the next scene in communication or decision-making. Different people respond differently in a given situation; depending on various factors - social, cultural, educational, age and experience-related awareness, data-related responses etc. In business too our response would be based on these very same factors, however mental maturity plays a very crucial role in our response-pattern.

Many people confuse reaction with response. Reaction is an almost involuntary knee-jerk action where as a response would be a conscious activity. When the conscious mind is involved, the nature of response would be more poised and well thought out .The consequences of such responses would be positive and meaningful.

Sometimes silence and non-reaction is also a response. This reminds me of a saying "No response is the loudest of all". As we know action leads to response; our positive actions get us positive responses.

8 SELF-PEP-TALK

We all talk to ourselves, some do it in silence, some do it aloud, some call it thinking, some do it to gain confidence and some do it for courage. Some people feel comfortable talking to themselves, and for some it is a way out for loneliness.

Self-talk has a lot of positive implications in our mind, it can boost confidence and self esteem. Self-talk is also used in health care to treat many psychological challenges. It is proved that self-pep-talk can vitalise our lives, it is this power of self-talk that has made many sports men create new records.

Even in our day to day life when we require brainstorming self-talk is worth trying. It could also help in finding creative solution to difficult problems.

To start a self talk we should be able to recognise the self within us and treat that self as another conscious individual; it may be difficult in the beginning but not impossible, once we are able to achieve this, we can start thinking aloud. It is like having an optimistic voice in our head that always looks at the brighter side.

9 INVESTING TIME

Investment need not always mean money, even time is an investment. We could invest in relationships, knowledge, assets etc. No investment is a waste. These investments will go a long way in our professional and personal life.

Investing Time

We are often judged by our wise investments. The more we invest in relationship and knowledge, the better empowered we will be as a person or as a professional. So be a wise investor.

"You'll never have control over other people's decisions, or what cards life deals you. Your power lies in the choosing of your response. That is the one thing you can control."

-JohnMarkGreen-

10 VALUE OF TIME

Once the great Mugal Emperor Akbar asked Birbal his minister, "What is the most valuable thing on this earth?" Birbal replied 'It's Time, my lord, because no amount of money can buy back lost time". Time is one of the valuable gifts God has equally distributed to each individual each day, irrespective of age, sex, class or religion. Very few people understand the value of this gift. Time is very precious because everything in this world is acquired in time. We should use time in the best possible manner because we cannot enjoy even the best things if we do not have time for it. One should always value another's time as much as one's own.

Time & Money

A good leader is always on time. You must have observed that right timing is the secret of all successful ventures.

11 BEING AS EXAMPLE

Leading by example is important. This is easier said than done. Very few leaders can walk the talk. However, successful leaders are mindful of their actions and practice what they preach. A leader is accountable to his team and he should always be aware that he is being watched and is in the public domain of his team.

The leader shall set examples of excellence.

12 FACING PROBLEMS HEAD ON

Problems are part and parcel of everyday life. Look at problems as challenges.

Real leaders take on issues head on and they know how to discover the root of the problem. They take charge and act. Leaders do not procrastinate , instead they pull up their socks and get to the root of matter. They never avoid uncomfortable situations.

Be a successful leader, get ahead, face challenges head on.

13 CHALLENGE TO THINK

Successful leaders understand their Team like the back of their palm. They know the mindset and capabilities of each member of their team. Leaders use this knowledge to challenge their team to think, stretch and to achieve professional and personal goals.

Such knowledge will also help the leader in devising strategies, which will inspire his team to accept new challenges.

A leader is dependable and trustworthy.

CHALLENGE TO THINK

KISHORE

14 REWARD

A leader is successful because of his team and he knows it very well.

However, very few managers know the art of appreciation. A true leader understands the importance of appreciation. He gives due credit to the individuals responsible for achieving a particular objective. Appreciation and reward go a long way in keeping any individual motivated.

Reward

The timing of the reward is equally important. It should be given as soon as possible. There is no place for delay here. Such simple acts of a leader inspire the team to achieve greater heights.

15 COMMITMENT

Commitment marks out the professional among ordinary people. It is always a big challenge to find people with commitment. Only people with commitment are dependable and they are the ones whom we can trust.

Before we look for commitment in others it is always better to introspect on ourselves. Did I ever break a promise? Have I always kept my word? Did I always complete promised tasks without reminders?

Positive answers to these questions will be few. This means it is time to change our attitude.

Commitment

16 EVALUATION

Evaluation is a word often heard in management discussions. Evaluation is making a judgement about the people, amount, number or value of something. In one word, it is assessment (vis-à-vis a set standard).

We claim expertise in evaluating others. People don't miss any opportunity to evaluate others; they are often judgemental too. To understand evaluation: "it is a systematic determination of a subject's merit, worth and significance, using criteria governed by a set of standards". Let us be judicious while evaluating others because everyone has his own reasons for acting in a certain way. Let us appreciate that.

The best way of assessment is to put oneself in the other man's situation

17 PLANING

Good planning is at the root of any successful project. If we do not plan, we are exposing ourselves to surprises, which need not be pleasant every time. Planning need not be restricted to organisations, every individual must plan for success in life.

Our objective is to get positive results; so why hesitate to plan? Never stick to a single plan, we must have multiple plans for contingencies, only then we can expect desired results.

18 INNOVATION

Innovation happens only if we dare to question the conventional. Innovators have a very different dimension for looking at things. Think of the innovator who designed meeting-hall chairs on the lines of arrangement of leaves in a cabbage. A hundred chairs can be kept one within the other and easily carried to distant places!

We are social animals with herd mentality .We all like to be in crowds and take beaten paths.

If you follow the herd you too will reach where the herd would reach. To conquer new heights one should move away from the crowd sometimes and take the untrodden path. Change is painful but innovators are willing to take that pain in order to create something new.

All innovations may not be blockbusters, however, we must continue to innovate because the future belongs to innovators.

19 JUGAAD INNOVATION

Jugaad Innovation is also known as frugal innovation. This kind of an innovation may look foolish but when we look deep, we can find brilliance behind such creativity. Jugaad innovation specifically addresses 'the need' rather than "the want". This requires unconventional and out-of-the-box thinking. The greatest and the most recent jugaad innovation is the successful *Mangal Yaan* mission of ISRO, this mission was successful in putting a satellite in the orbit of Mars using earth's gravitation to catapult the satellite at a fraction of the international cost. The word jugaad in Hindi means innovative or lateral fixes or a simple work-around or some kind of adjustments to make a low-cost solution. Let us remember that the output of a jugaad innovation is always a workable solution at very low cost.

A *Jugaad innovation* is making most out of what you have. It focus on needs rather than wants.

The most important aspect of Jugaad innovation is cost effective outputs. A few examples of Jugaad innovations we see around us are the reuse of cola bottles as water bottles, burning of used mosquito repellent mats to drive away mosquitoes effectively, making "country trucks" using parts of bullock carts with water pumps as engines etc. The basic method for producing Jugaad Innovations are 1) a proper understanding of the problem 2) understanding of principles of the conventional solutions 3) finding a solution away from conventional methods 4) thinking of wild solutions 5) thinking of simple methods 6) looking for readily available resources 7) exploring all alternatives 8) creating a solution at 10 percent of the current solution cost 9) seeking help from people of outside industries 10) keeping complications away and looking for basics.

20 OPEN TO IDEAS

Great ideas often come from the most unlikely sources. In fact, many ideas do not get recognised because they have originated from unconventional sources.

We all are confident about our own knowledge and skill, so we find it very difficult to accept ideas from people or sources which are not familiar to us. This is because of human ego and our presumptions create a big wall between us and the idea.

Recently a friend of mine who is into an electronic trading business lost a big corporate order for 20,000 laptops, because he refused to take the help of his nephew, as he could not believe or accept that his 24 year old nephew could have contacts in the board. The order was bagged by a competitor through the same boy's connection.

OPEN TO IDEAS

We must keep eyes and ears open for ideas and opportunities, they can come in any form. The Rig Veda says 'Let noble thoughts come to us from every side'.

21 THE KID IN YOU

You'd agree that the most creative, are children. They have the ability to visualise without boundaries. And beyond those boundaries lies the realm of innovation. Ideas generated without prejudice would be different from the conventional thinking; children are gifted to do it. Each one of us have a child within us and as we grow old our adult ego would suppress that little kid forever.

Imagination and creativity comes naturally to children, so let's try to look at things as if we are a 5-year old and we would have a totally new world around us. If we wake up the child within us, our life would turn positive, full of energy and surprises. We would find many occasions to wonder at little things, so let the child in us make our life fascinating and creative.

22 CRISIS MANAGEMENT

We all must have faced a crisis at some point of time in our life and many of us may have handled it successfully.

Crisis management is the process by which any organisation or individual manages major events which can threaten the smooth functioning of a system.

Lack of proper and timely management of a crisis can lead to chaos. The challenge lies in the ability to find the right solution to a demanding situation in time. In a crisis, be calm and approach it systematically.

CRISIS

KISHORE

One should use knowledge wisely and seek help if needed. One of the easiest ways of facing a crisis is to recall a similar situation in the past and how it was solved. That takes away all tension from your mind and prepares you to face the crisis.

23 BEING A SALESMAN

Every day we interact with many people. There is exchange of words and gestures and this is communication. Have you ever realised that you are 'selling' many times with each interaction?

When we communicate we often try to convince others about our ideas, thoughts, needs, opinions, views etc. It is nothing but an effort to sell. Once we start treating others with respect as we treat our business clients, our language will be polite, our faces will lit up with smiles and body emit positive gestures. The result of such interaction could be amazing.

SALESMAN

24 DREAMING SUCCESS

Everyone enjoys success in every activity one does. Success is a feeling of accomplishment.

Some people are always successful. They have a special way of looking at things, they look at things positively. Small failures do not affect them for they take lessons from them.

Always look for positive results from every activity you do. A positive result is called success. You should dream success from every project. The visualisation itself will bring in positive energy into the venture and you will be able to reap success.

26 TRANSPERANCY

Have you ever enjoyed working with incomplete information? Everyone likes to work towards a known goal. Working with incomplete information is very difficult. It is always better to have transparency with your team mates, so that they understand what they are working for. Let them enjoy the fruits of success.

This happens when there is transparency in communication. When all members of the team know what they are working for, their commitment to the completion of the task will be greater.

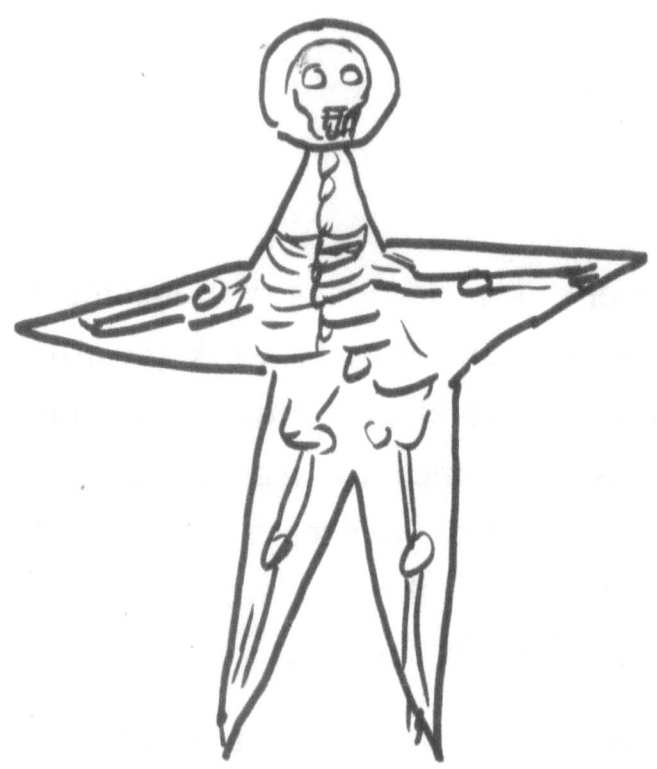

Transparent Leader

A transparent leader will win the trust of his subordinates and he can build a committed team.

27 BE UPDATED

The world is changing at a fast pace. What was relevant yesterday is history today and what is relevant today will become obsolete tomorrow. We don't even look the same after 5 years. We must   accept change as a norm and move in tandem with change. This is possible only if we update ourselves with new skills, knowledge & modern technology.

Well-informed people are accepted everywhere. Change is difficult but it is worth taking that pain in order to move with the times.

We should be future- ready or be left behind to become irrelevant history.

28 EMOTIONS

We believe that decisions are based on logical observation but studies have proved that 80% of decisions are made purely on emotions. Ability to understand other's emotions will make one a successful   leader.
Most human interaction is governed by sense rather than logic. People are often judged by their   EQ   rather   than   their   IQ.
It is better to rule over hearts rather than heads because the heart understands the unique language of love, care & empathy.

29 INTEGRITY

In today's world it is easy to find people with great academic accomplishments but the chances of finding people with integrity are extremely rare. Success comes and goes but integrity remains forever. A person with integrity will be remembered with respect even after his death. Integrity means doing the right thing at all times and in all circumstances. It takes great courage to do only the right thing always irrespective of the consequences. It takes ages to build integrity but one wrong step can damage it, so one must be extremely careful about one's deeds. Let us put in conscious effort to develop integrity within us.

30 CALCULATED RISK

We all have taken risks at some points of time in our lives and tasted success or failure as the result   of   our   risk-taking. No business can grow without some amount of risk- taking. Every entrepreneur takes risks. The successful ones are those who take calculated risks.

The safest way to survive is by not taking any risk, but then it is only survival. No progress or growth can happen if everyone gets complacent in his or her present position. Calculated risk understands the chance of failure, the probability of which is estimated before any action is taken. Once there is a clear understanding of the end result, the path can be redefined to increase the chance of success. Take calculated risks in life, it's worth the effort.

31 FOCUS

The secret of achieving any objective is the ability to focus solely on the target like Arjuna* did when he saw only the eye of the toy bird. No objective can be achieved unless we know clearly what the objective is all about and the path to reach there.

In today's hi-tech world there are so many gizmos to distract us, like the smart phone. How do we focus when our brain is too eager to attend to these modern day toys and other attention diverters? There are no shortcuts, we should be able to set our priorities and know when to put off these diverters into silent mode. Focussing is possible with meditation; meditation is constant thought of something when the time gap between two thoughts tends to zero.

*A great warrior, character from the epic Mahabharata

32 AT WHAT COST?

To reach the top we always use the fastest mode available. When we look back we can see a number of people we have pushed behind on our way to the top. We always do have our own reasons and would never want to compromise. We should realise that the credit of our success does not belong to us alone. There would be many others who have helped us up on our journey to the top. When we push for results, let us ask ourselves if the end is a realistic one and what it would cost to achieve it.

33 FACING CRITICISM

Criticism fails many successful people who do not know how to handle failure. When one is in the growth-path, one should be prepared to face criticism. Criticism is critical analysis and evaluation of something. When one does new things different from conventional norms, there will be people with difference of opinion. When one has critics, it is an opportunity to look at areas which one wasn't aware of. It also helps one to fine-tune one's ways and to introspect on one's path. One must take criticism in the positive stride like a bitter pill for cure. The source doesn't matter as long as one knows how to use criticism to one's benefit, to accelerate one's growth..

34 FAITH

Let's look at each goal as a destination and in this journey we face both success and failure. A normal person would celebrate success and feel sorry when he fails. A leader is different, he moves on till the goal is achieved. He does not stay contented with small success or grieve at failures. The journey to achieve great goals has many hurdles and each hurdle should only make him sharpen his skill to stretch and leap. As the leader moves ahead his team is with him and that makes his job more responsible. It is this faith in him that keeps the team going. Faith is not developed overnight; it takes great effort and time to build it. The leader should take every effort to keep the faith of his team in him. Once lost he can never get it back.

35 HAPPINESS

Everyone works to achieve happiness. It is the end objective of every deed. Often people have happiness of the self as their goal. There are some who work for others' happiness and they emerge as true leaders. Happiness is a state of mind. One can achieve this by simply modifying the way one looks at life. It's like the half-glass-empty or half-glass-full theory. You can decide to be happy from any position, by simply looking at your achievements and blessings. At the same time when you look at the road ahead you cannot enjoy the journey till you reach your destination. If you can enjoy the journey itself you will realise a new dimension of happiness.

The choice is yours, it is better to appreciate your own achievement once in a while and be happy about it.

understanding of the end result, the path can be redefined to increase the chance of success. Take calculated risks in life, it's worth the effort.

36 ENERGY INVESTMENT

It is very important to know where one should focus one's energy. It is the energy that we invest which gets converted into promising results. Worrying about the past or future can only create anxiety and thus the energy gets wasted. The intelligent way of using one's energy is to invest it in the present and do everything in the best possible manner.

Energy is not physical alone, it includes different resources like technology, finance, experts, market opportunity and many more. We should be able to direct all the energy or resources to the core objective and we'll find miracles delivered.

37 OWNING RESPONSIBILITY

When there is success the sailing is smooth and there's rejoicing everywhere. Everybody loves to take credit for success. It is said success has many fathers and failure is an orphan. The successful team becomes vibrant and there is a feeling of oneness. The leader gets credit for the team's achievement; he gives due credit to his team mates for their contribution.

But it is failure that will test the real mettle of the team leader. Failure breaks the morale of the team and they have only their leader to lean on. Such a debacle is a challenge to the leader. A true leader will own the responsibility of the failure and not look for scapegoats. He remembers that the team is his strength. To recall former President Abdul Kalam's experience: When an SLV launch failed (when he was project director) the ISRO chairman

Mr. Satish Dhawan addressed the press saying

they had failed. Next time when the launch was a success the chairman asked Mr Kalam (project director) to call and address the press conference.

One's philosophy is not best expressed in words; it is expressed in the choices one makes... and the choices we make are ultimately our responsibility.
–Eleanor.Roosevelt-

38 NOURISH BUSINESS RELATIONSHIP

Relationships do not develop on their own, it takes sincere efforts to develop and retain relationships. In our day to day professional and personal life we come across tens of thousands of people.
Often we hardly remember those we had met a couple of years ago; we do not feel the need for it. In today's world nobody wants to keep a contact unless he feels the need for it. If one makes a conscious effort to give due attention and importance to the people with whom one interacts, to let them feel important, the results can be astonishing.

39 WHAT IS YOUR USP

Have you ever realised that you are a special edition? Yes, there is no other person like you in this whole world of 7.4 billion people. God has taken so much care to make each one of us special. Then why are we following others, like members of a herd? We all have some unique quality that can make us stand out from the rest. We need to identify it and work on it. This unique quality can become our USP. In any business or occupation, we must look for areas where we can make a difference with our unique skill. The world is in need of people with original ideas; there are millions of copy cats. It takes conscious effort to be unique, make a mark in whatever one does, to let one's signature be engraved there.

40 CELEBRATE LIFE

We have just one life and we have a choice to live it our way. We can make our lives spicy, glamorous, pious, carefree or even work-weary. It is very difficult to choose from various life options available. A corporate management professional lives life working all day for his company's profits to boom and stocks to zoom. He gains the reputation of a very hard working executive totally committed to his organisation. If you ask his family, you will get a very different picture. He may be getting a big pay cheque, but at what cost? He will realise his loss only when he retires, by which time life would have passed by leaving him too old and weak to enjoy life. We must take care not to lose out on life itself and miss its beauties during our journey to professional success. We need to celebrate life when we are in control and lead a balanced life. Only we can prioritise options in our life.

41 WINNING ATTITUDE

It is attitude that makes or breaks a person, it decides how an individual would respond to any given situation. Nothing can stop the man with a winning attitude from achieving his goals. Our words can only be heard, but it is the attitude that others can feel. It is a silent communicator that determines your body language.

Sir Winston Churchill once said "Attitude is a little thing that can make a big difference" You may have large goals and big dreams but it is the attitude that determines how well you work towards them. If we make a promise to ourselves that we shall always have a positive attitude and we will enjoy positive results for the rest of our life.

42 FAILURE IS NOT A VILLAIN

The taste of success is always sweet; none of us ever wants to taste failure. Accepting failure is very difficult. We do not believe that failure is also a possibility. We start all activities with success in mind, which is positive thinking. Anticipating a possibility of failure is not negative thinking. Our approach to failure is what makes the difference. Failure is not the end, just time for another beginning.

Failure teaches us many lessons. There are numerous opportunities hidden in a failure, analysing each failure can open doors to new lessons which cannot be learned otherwise. Our plan B or plan C should have areas where these lessons can be used for improvement. Believing that failure is just another possibility and moving forward with the lessons learnt is the right thing to do.

43 BE ALONE WITH YOURSELF

It is the inner voice that communicates the truth. It knows what is right and what is wrong. The day we befriend our inner self we will find many doors opening for us. When there is darkness everywhere, we can still find light within us to guide us on our path. It is this conscience which many of us neglect in our quest for success and growth. Our true friend is within us. Listening to our heart, we shall be able to solve many complex problems which would not be manageable otherwise.

The world's greatest business ideas have not come from big management institutes but from intuitions.

Let us spend quality time with ourselves and listen to our heart; we would make no mistake.

44 TRAVEL WITH OPEN MIND

Remaining an island will never give us any worthy exposure. In the ancient times the learned were those who travelled wide and met rare tribes. European explorers were instrumental in making access to this huge wide world possible. When we travel we often restrict our travel to our pre-planned agenda, seldom do we break away from our itinerary to explore new places or interact freely with strangers. We avoid unknown people, it is because we all seek the cushion of comfort and fear the unknown. Knowledge is everywhere in abundance. It is up to us to grab it. Every place we travel to and every person we meet has so much to offer.

Let's face the unknown with an open mind, who knows big opportunities might be waiting for us to explore and exploit!.

Arise! awake! approach the great and learn. like the sharp edge of a razor is that path, so the wise say—hard to tread and difficult to cross.

— Katha Upanishad-

45 HUMILITY

Today's success does not guarantee a successful future. There are various factors that contribute to our success. The most important of them is human resource power. If we analyse each success story, we will be able to identify many people who claimed no credit for their contribution. Once we realise this truth about others' effort and sacrifices for our success, we would feel humbled. Let success not go to our head, each success should be a burden on our shoulder. We should be indebted to the many known and unknown helping, steadying hands for our achievements. As one rises up the career ladder one realises the limitations of each higher position. All great men are simple and humble, this is because they know their limitations and responsibilities. *'Vidya vinayena shobhate'*- knowledge shines through humility.

Success is a gift for our hard work, patience and humility. As the saying goes "Don't judge your day by the harvest you reap, but by the seeds you plant."

The wise man beholds all beings in the self and the self in all beings; for that reason he does not hate anyone. – isa Upanishad

46 IMPART KNOWLEDGE

The knowledge that we possess is a gift given to us by our parents, teachers, friends, well- wishers and the society at large. Nature itself has given us knowledge in abundance. It is our responsibility to share it with others .The more we share, the better we are enriched. We do not have ownership of knowledge as it is only acquired from others and we should consider it as a gift from our well wishers.

We should show equal zeal to impart this knowledge to others as we had the enthusiasm to acquire it. Knowledge gets stagnant if it is not updated or imparted. So we should use all available means to update our knowledge, otherwise we will become anachronisms.

47 BE A HERO

We all agree that a leader is a hero to his team and he is their role model. If it is so, will we not agree on the importance of his presentation of self? Each one of us is a brand and we all have our own unique identity. This is true with the way we look, the way we dress, the way we behave etc. Just like that of any consumer product our packaging is equally important. We all know the importance of perception. As mentioned earlier, 80 percentage of assessments are made subjectively, based on emotions mostly created by perception. Self-presentation package consists of * our attire, * our looks (hair and grooming), *the gadgets we use, *our visiting card, *the confidence in our approach,*positive body gestures,* quality of communication,*our mannerisms,*our contacts etc.

All the above should be consciously balanced and managed or it could lead to confusion.

We need not bother about any of the above points if we have a super strong iconic personality like that of Mahatma Gandhi or Mother Teresa.

Excellence is an art won by training and habituation. We do not act rightly because we have virtue or excellence, but we rather have those because we have acted rightly. We are what we repeatedly do. Excellence, then, is not an act but a habit.

-Aristotle-

48 BE PASSIONATE

The one common ingredient which all successful people share is their passion towards what they do. They are very passionate about their job, business or profession.

When we add passion to our work, we never feel that we are working, since our job becomes our hobby and we never get tired of pursuing our hobby.

Passion makes work easy and enjoyable, bringing in creativity. Once we are passionate about the work, we do not need anyone to supervise, we become our own boss because we have taken ownership of the task.

Passion is love towards something. We can be passionate about anything only if we love it. Hence whatever we do let's try to reason out, what we like about it and why we should enjoy doing it. Once we identify *that one reason*, we can develop passion towards it.

49 BACK TO BASICS

Life has become complex. Everywhere we find complex technology, principles, rules, values, gizmos etc. This has led us into a world which is like a jigsaw puzzle. Today freedom of expression is also compromised and we have to be very careful with each word we utter, because we do not know which statement of ours could trigger unrest in any particular group of people.

Religion was once considered very personal and sacred, but now this too has become very complicated with different people interpreting differently according to their convenience to create confusions. Party politics makes its presence everywhere - the education system, company managements – all have got entangled in unnecessary complications leading to confusion in our minds. We have become too cautious even with our thinking.

When such complex situations arise either in

personal or professional life, the best option is to go back to the basics. There you find solutions to all complex problems.

The energy of the mind is the essence of life.

- Aristotle-

50 PROCASTINATION

The word procrastination is viewed as a negative one, people who procrastinate are considered lazy.

Let's understand procrastination, it is the act or habit of putting off or delaying urgent and important task and giving importance for doing less important, enjoyable and less challenging work. Procrastination is a habit which should be done away with as it destroys the professionalism of the individual. People who do not pay attention to important and urgent matters are never respected in professional circles, they are considered casual and non- serious types.

A professional should always give importance and priority to matters that require immediate attention at the same time he should have a clear plan for other activities too. He should develop the skill of prioritizing without diluting the importance of tasks at the fag end of the list.

51 ADAPTABILITY

Change is the unchanging law of life. This makes the world dynamic. Dynamism is seen in every field. The simple magic formula one could follow successfully in dynamic situations is adaptation. We should be able to adapt to any given situation. In every environment there is change. In organizations people change, the nature of job could change or market conditions might change. This is the time when one should embrace adaptability. We should accept change as a norm and put conscious effort to adapt to the given situation. Accepting the change itself is half the job done, the balance will come from our conscious efforts. It would be wise not to resist change because we would be powerless trying to move against time. The best way to succeed in a changing situation is by being part of the change and that is the need of the hour.

52 THE COMPANY WE KEEP

We are social animals, we prefer to be part of specific socio-economic groups. Those groups are our company. In school, at the work place, in clubs or associations we seek a set group of people with whom we feel comfortable. On analysing, we would understand that our company mostly consists of people with our own tastes / interest .As the saying goes, 'Birds of a feather flock together'.

Peer pressure has a great role to play in our growth. This peer group is our company. We can observe that great men always keep the company of great people. Creative minds choose creative people for company, businessmen have friends from business contacts, the same is true of intellectuals, bureaucrats, politicians etc. We can also put ourselves on a different level/ footing if we are careful about choosing the company we keep. The company of positive and energetic people will make our lives vibrant. Our conscious decision on the company we keep will decide our destiny.

For a man to conquer himself is the first and noblest of all victories.
—Plato-

53 JUNK IN THE INFORMATION HIGHWAY

We are on a fast moving information highway, where there is no dearth of knowledge, what is required is our will to be choosy. How much of this knowledge will be of use to us? Every information is available online and at our finger tips. Yet we seem information-starved.

The real challenge is in filtering the available data to get the right information. We should be able to distinguish between the useful and the useless. There is no point in gathering information inputs that are irrelevant to us. This is often waste of time, yet we try to capture the details of unimportant information.

 Social media claim to be information warehouses; are they really worth their claim? Have we ever wondered how much junk we absorb for the sake of a little knowledge? How often have we tried to move out of such junk? The spicy stuff will get us glued to this media.

Only our strong determination can help us get out of this maze.

54 UNDERSTANDING ENTREPRENEURSHIP

Entrepreneurs are people like you and me; many of them may not even have proper education, yet there is something in them that makes them different and outstanding.

The most important quality entrepreneurs possess is their ability to dream and visualise success. They win the race in their minds much before the real race begins. They are not afraid of failures and are willing to take many risks, as failures do not break them. They evolve stronger after each debacle.

They like to get their hands dirty, they work their way up. They are knowledgeable about their customers, financers, suppliers etc. and spend quality time in creating business relationships.

Entrepreneurs value time, they understand the importance of right timing, and they value the time of all their stakeholders. If we want to be successful entrepreneurs we should be able to create trustworthy teams to whom we can delegate important assignments.

The entrepreneurs' is a big responsibility as they are also helping in nation-building by creating employment opportunities. Entrepreneurs are innovators too.

55 LOOK BACK

Growth is the sign of life, and each one of us is in the fast track competing with many others.

The ambition for growth and pace has made us aggressive in our mission. We are taught to aim high to set goals and create strategy to reach them.

Our vision should be clear as our path, we do not stop at obstacles or challenges. We are determined to accept nothing less than success.

We are never willing to look back once on the race track. Unlike sports, life offers many lessons on this track.

It is advisable to look back once in a while and revisit our path, we would find answers to many of our tricky questions. Remember our path and look ahead; success will follow.

56 SCALABILITY

Scalability is a term we usually come across with reference to the IT industry. According to Wikipedia scalability is the ability of a system, network or process to handle a growing amount of work in a capable manner or its ability to be enlarged to accommodate that growth. This is a clear definition apt for a software or hardware product.

Should we restrict the concept of scalability to Information Technology alone? Wouldn't you agree that this process can be effectively implemented in the life of every human being? We live in an era of rapid changes and fast growth, everything around us transforms faster than our imagination. Whatever skill and knowledge we acquire becomes obsolete very fast.

What we need today is the ability to accommodate this change and we should be able to be the part of this change process. We should also be able to bring in scalability in our skill, knowledge and contacts.

The requirement of tomorrow cannot be met with yesterday's skill.

57 WALK THE TALK

The most challenging question a leader could face is "Sir, would you do it? It may sound strange but the fact is, most of the business leaders and trainers do not practice all that they preach. We often see very successful trainers seldom follow what they advise in their classes. Such trainers or leaders would lose their credibility in the long run.

WALK THE TALK

In business the best way to protect ourselves from a false promise is by documenting it with an email confirmation. Once the verbal communication gets confirmed with an email, there is very little chance for denial. In case of dispute or misunderstanding of any kind, we might receive an email reply accordingly. In both cases our interest would be protected.

While we are in the leadership position ensure

that we honour our commitments. We have to be extremely careful while giving commitments to others; we should only promise what we can deliver, at the same time never expect others to remind us about the promises we made.

Once a promise is made, then it becomes our responsibility to deliver.

58 FREEDOM

A true leader knows the importance of privacy of his team-mates and he never trespasses into their area of operation unless they seek his help.

He has confidence in the ability of his team. Innovation will evolve when people are given freedom to perform. Good planning and timely allocation of responsibility to the team would avoid urgency and fire fighting.

Let your teammates feel comfortable in your presence. Try to be the part of the solution and not the problem.

The leader should be a motivator rather than a monitor. Remember how "Jambavan motivated Hanuman to jump across the ocean to Lanka when all other team-mates expressed inability"*.

Let your team not work for you. Let them work with you for reaching a goal.

*An incident from the Hindu epic Ramayan

59 CRITICISM IS GOOD

Everyone cannot face criticism with ease; we should understand that criticism is also a reaction we have to face when our performance is subjected to another's scrutiny. We should be open to accept different reactions when we interact with people. Some reactions make us happy; some make us think and some reactions would even break us. Criticism is one such reaction; if not taken in the right prospective it could destroy our confidence. When we are criticised the best way is to accept it as a feedback from that person to our performance and take it as an opportunity to improve. One may even thank the criticiser for his frank views!

When Sugreeva got back his kingdom with Sri Rama's help he spent days in enjoying life with drinks and women forgetting the word given to Sri Rama to search for Sitadevi. One day his minister Hanuman reminded him of his promise and told him it is better to remember that the same arrow that killed Bali is still with Sri Rama.

Sugreeva came to senses and said a king with such a minister will never fail.*

An incident from the Hindu epic Ramayan

Criticism is good ???

Criticisms on performance must always be welcome, especially when it is constructive. Criticising the performer is another dimension of response, which is not encouraged in management of persons or business.

Any fool can criticize, condemn, and complain but it takes character and self control to be understanding and forgiving.

-Dale Carnegie-

60 FUTURE READY

How many of us are confident of the future? Are we future-ready? These are difficult questions to answer because hardly anybody can predict future; how can one be future-ready? That is the challenge. Future-ready means equipping ourselves ready to meet the requirement of future, this can be achieved by acquiring skill, knowledge and attitude for tomorrow. Lot of homework is required to understand the trend of today which might hold some secret about tomorrow. We cannot avoid this activity as there is no point in doing something, which has no relevance for future. When we invest in business, knowledge, technology, education etc.

it is very important that we understand its future implications and requirements. Our knowledge about future would help us re-align all our activities. Don't go blind into the future, have some idea as to what is in store there. Only our preparation would enable us to have a peep into the future.

"Life can only be understood backwards; but it must be lived,forwards."

— *Soren Kierkegaard* -

61 POWER OF SILENCE

At times silence is more powerful than a strong word. Silence has the in-built ability to convey a message better, which even a large sentence cannot. The secret lies in the ability and skill with which one uses silence. On some occasions silence can convey a whole lot of emotions.

In written communication, responding to unpleasant mails often pumps more emotions than what is required, and the best way to reduce emotions in our reply is not to reply immediately, and wait for a day before we reply. A pause or silence of one day would change the mood of our reply.

POWER OF SILENCE

Many of us do not know the art of silence, we know to speak for hours on many topics but when it comes to silence we find it difficult to use it to our advantage. Let's understand the power of silence and use it in the best possible manner. In legal studies there is a usage, "when silence is equivalent to speaking".

62 SELF MOTIVATION

Motivation is power that is required for any action to take place. Different people have different needs, fulfilment of these needs are their motivators. Some get motivated by money, some by recognition, and some by life style change. For some people it is satisfaction of physiological needs that motivates them. There could be many more motivating factors.

We spend a lot of time and resources, trying to analyse and understand the motivational requirement of our subordinates, colleagues, family, friends etc. How many of us have identified our self motivational factors; do we know what keeps us going, can we identify that one key element that helps us stretch? If we know that, we can walk that extra mile with ease; with the right kind of self-motivating tools we can make many unpleasant work enjoyable.

To motivate is easy, but to keep one motivated for a longer period is difficult. It is possible through self-motivation, when the leader becomes a model worth emulating.

If one advances confidently in the direction of his dreams, and endeavours to live the life which he has imagined, he will meet with success unexpected in common hours.

-Henry David Thoreau-

63 RESPECT NATURE

In this commercial world, there is a price for everything we use. We pay for good life, education, housing, electricity, fuel, and the list goes on. When it comes to nature, it gives us everything in abundance and does not even charge us a penny. We human beings exploit this wonderful nature for our own selfish wants without any consideration. We should remember that the day nature starts billing us for sunlight and oxygen, the whole of human race would go bankrupt within a day.

It is our responsibility to take care of nature and respect its resources .We only have limited right to use natural resources. We have no right to abuse it. Whatever activity we do, we should check for its impact on nature and ensure that we do not do anything that hurts the delicate balance. This earth belongs to Future generations too.

64 MENTOR

Mentor is like a coach or guide, he or she should be a person with vast experience and exposure. Having a mentor would be helpful in understanding new and challenging developments of any industry.

Let's understand why it is important to have a mentor; a right mentor would be your Guru and he would impart immense knowledge which he has acquired over years of toil and learning. We cannot learn everything from colleges or colleagues, where as a mentor would hold keys to many professional secrets which might enlighten us.

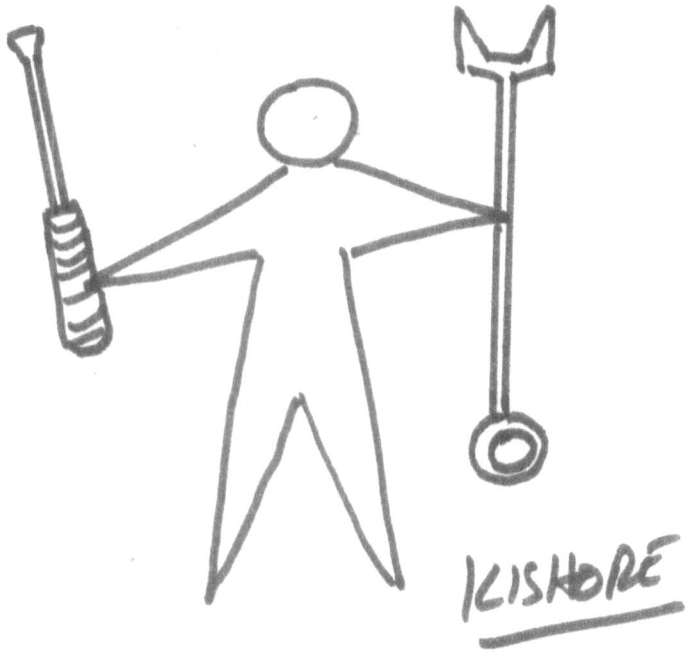

The

mentor

Remember we cannot choose our mentor, we should be chosen, spend quality time with people who are more knowledgeable and experienced than us. Who knows, we might find our mentor in them.

65 THE GURU

Who is a Management Guru? We might think that a management guru is an authority on the subject, but then he should be called a learned man, why call him guru?

A guru is an unquestioned person of his realm. Wisdom pervades all his activities. He is a repository of knowledge and shares it with all those who seek knowledge.

Haven't you heard of this? "A young guru was sitting beneath a tree. Old disciples were sitting around him. The guru did not utter a word. But the disciples understood everything." True wisdom makes thought transference.

If we use these parameters to identify a Management guru, then it would be a big challenge even to find a single person who qualifies to be a guru.

In today's world nobody shares knowledge free and no one has time for others. They forget their past, they forgot the source of their basic knowledge and they only think of earning money for every minute they spend with others. Monetary gains overrule ethics and principles.

Still if you could find a management guru,

you would be a very lucky person. Search, you will find!

66 SPECIALISATION

We all do have some unique ability or skill and we are better at it. When it comes to professional excellence, we are in the era of super specialisation. We not only have specialist in each field but there are super specialists who have extra knowledge in their specified area.

We have the freedom of choice whether to be a specialist or super specialist or for that matter even a jack of all trades. This depends on individual likes and traits. An expert is one who knows more and more about less and less.

The need of the hour is people with multiple specialisation, this can be achieved by specialisation in a particular area and then diversifying knowledge and skill into other areas under the same domain. The domain specific diversification is needed. Thus we can have multiple specialisation in a particular domain. This will keep us alert, updated and open to new knowledge.

"When you compete with a person, you only have to be as good or better than the
person to win. If you compete with yourself, there is no limitation to how good you can be."

-CHUCHIN-NING-

67 FEAR AND ANXIETY

Little fear and anxiety is what keeps us moving forward. No growth is possible without self motivation and here comes the role of anxiety, which will ensure that we do things perfect, because fear of failure will help us prepare well.

Fear is an emotion, induced by a threat perception; it is a vital response to physical and emotional danger. The feeling of fear is what keeps us prepared to face challenges because in every challenge there is threat and once we are aware of this threat, we take all the required precautions and we go well prepared to meet the threat.

Understanding fear is what will help us win over it and at the same time use it to our advantage in our growth.

68 FRIENDS WE KEEP

Our friends played the most vital role during our growing years, they taught us leadership, goal setting, planning, value of relationship and many more complex management lessons through the games we played with them as kids.

With friends we can share our success and failure without any inhibition. True friends remain with us during our ups and downs, they expect nothing in return for their love and support. Friends are forever.

FRIENDS WE KEEP

In professional life it is very difficult, though not impossible, to find true friends; if you are lucky to get one, don't ever lose him.

69 HIRE AND FIRE

The most uncomfortable decision a manager may take in his career is the decision to fire a subordinate. One should realise that we are not firing the individual but we are moving a person away from the responsibility, which he is incapable of managing. We can avoid the firing scenario if we develop a good training system which could equip individuals with skills they are more comfortable with. If at all we find an individual is weak in any particular area in spite of training, we should not let him continue to work in that department as he would be more demotivated .The best would be to move him to another department or area of his interest, such movement would not only keep the employee motivated, he might turn out to be an asset to the organisation. Hiring is a challenge, as it is very difficult to predict employee commitment. While hiring, evaluate attitude and behaviour more than skill, because skills can be developed with good training.

70 PEOPLE AND CHANGE

For changes to happen in any organization, the first change should start at people level, which means the need of change and its importance should be felt by the people working in the organization; no change can be implemented successfully without the people's   involvement.

Before we initiate a change process in the organization, a proper orientation program should be initiated for the department-heads, which is then to be imparted to their respective   teams.

In   change-management   peer   pressure works wonders, hence the influencer and opinion leaders are to be involved and once they embrace change others would follow soon.

We should not bring in so many changes at one go, rather introduce one at a time and this will bring in seamless integration of new processes into the existing system.

71 SUBTRACT TO ADD

When we are on the growth highway lot of new things get added to us (in the process). When organizations grow we find new people joining, new machines get installed, technology gets upgraded, they get new suppliers etc. And the list goes on.

We as human beings are emotional and we get attached not only to people but also to many other things like furniture, vehicle, systems, processes etc.

Sometimes these attachments might become a baggage of burden. We need to identify dead logs and keep removing them from our inventory to accommodate new additions for growth.

Subtract is Add

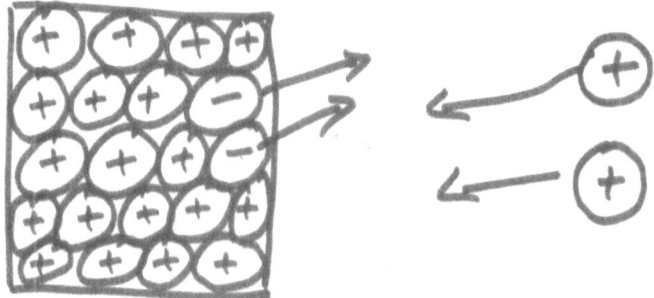

We should learn to unlearn before we learn new skills.

72 PEER PRESSURE

We all have experienced peer pressure since the day we were kids. In school we competed with each other and always tried to get ahead of our friends. This peer pressure can work wonders when we plan to implement new system into our organization.

Any change is viewed as a pain and nobody wants to adapt new system or processes or even technology. Only great amount of motivation can bring in change.

We were very comfortable with the keypads on our phones but we moved to touch screen. More than technological advantage it is peer pressure that made us change.

Peer Pressure

Whenever we plan to bring in change into an organization involve leaders and influencers; once they accept a new system, convincing others would be easy.

Like the butter hidden in milk, the pure consciousness resides in every being; that ought to be constantly churned out by the churning rod of the mind.

-Amrita-Bindu Upanishad-